GIANT PANDAS

GIANT PANDAS

Kay McDearmon

A SKYLIGHT BOOK

Illustrated with photographs

DODD, MEAD & COMPANY
New York

PHOTOGRAPH CREDITS

Neg. No. 314801 (Photo: Julius Kirschner) Courtesy Department
Library Services, American Museum of Natural History, page 17;
Department of the Interior, Bureau of Sports Fisheries & Wildlife,
11; Los Angeles Zoo Photo by Neal Johnston, 23, 27, 28; National
Zoological Park, Smithsonian Institution, 10, 40, 41, 55, 58; National
Zoological Park, Smithsonian Institution by Ilene Berg, 31; © New
York Zoological Society Photo, 36; San Francisco Examiner, Photo
by Fran Ortiz, 42, 44; Heidi Schroeder, 2; World Wildlife Fund,
8, 52; World Wildlife Fund by Dr. George B. Schaller, 34, 47; ©
Zoological Society of San Diego, 22, 24, 50; © Zoological Society
of San Diego by Ron Garrison, 14.

Distributed in Canada by
McClelland and Stewart Limited, Toronto
Manufactured in the United States of America

1 2 3 4 5 6 7 8 9 10

Library of Congress Cataloging-in-Publication Data

McDearmon, Kay.
    Giant pandas.

    (A Skylight book)
    Includes index.
    Summary: Describes the characteristics and habits of
the giant panda, its life in the wild and in captivity,
efforts to hunt it and show it in zoos, and attempts to
save it as an endangered species.
    1. Giant panda—Juvenile literature. [1. Giant
panda. 2. Pandas. 7. Rare animals] I. Title.
QL737.C214M34 1986   599.74'443   85-20641
ISBN 0-396-08736-1

For Jeanie, Barbara, and Liz

CONTENTS

Pandas are round and cuddly looking.

1

A GIFT FROM CHINA

Everyone loves giant pandas—and no wonder. They're so round and cuddly looking, a bit like huge stuffed toys. With their black ears, noses, and eye patches they resemble clowns. And they are playful and fun to watch.

In this country you can see these black-and-white pandas only at the National Zoo in Washington, D.C. Should you catch Ling-Ling or Hsing-Hsing between naps, either could be doing headstands. Or Ling-Ling, the more active of the two, might be turning somersaults. On a hot summer day either panda could be sleeping on a block of ice.

If you're visiting the Panda House at mealtime, and

Hsing-Hsing (left) and Ling-Ling (right).

happen to be watching Ling-Ling, you may see her dump her food pan on her head after she finishes her dinner. She might also bat the pan around, as she did on her first day in her new home on April 16, 1972.

That day the two pandas had just been flown to

Musk-ox

Washington all the way from China on the other side of the world. President Richard Nixon, visiting China earlier that year, had promised to give two shaggy Arctic musk-ox to the Chinese. To show their pleasure, the Chinese offered this country a pair of giant pandas.

The Chinese prepared the animals for their long trip by taking them on trial flights. And when the pandas left China on a United States Air Force cargo plane, three Chinese experts were also on board to explain to keepers at the National Zoo how to care for the pandas.

So that the pandas would be comfortable in Panda House, their new home, it was air-conditioned to resemble the cool temperatures they were used to in China.

2

THE WORLD OF
THE GIANT PANDA

Today there are no giant pandas in the wild anywhere
except in small areas of central China. There the animals
live in bamboo jungles high in the rugged mountains.
Bamboo, a woody grass, looks more like a tree, and can
grow as high. Year-round the climate is damp and chilly,
with heavy rains in the summer and much snow in the
winter.

Once, long ago, the bamboo-eating giant panda could
find a home almost anywhere in the forests of eastern
China. Bamboo was plentiful, but over the years it began
to disappear. Since it must have moisture, when the
climate became drier the bamboo died out little by little.

Golden monkey

People also began cutting it down to make room for farms. So the panda had to keep moving to find enough food.

Pandas have always shared their mountain home with an abundance of wildlife. Beautiful blue-nosed golden monkeys fly through the trees. The cry of the cuckoo mingles with the lovely melody of the Chinese nightingale. And after dark many animals, including bears, packs of wild dogs, and an occasional leopard roam through the bamboo jungle.

3

HUNTING THE PANDA

For thousands of years the Chinese knew that the giant panda existed. But the Western World didn't discover it until 1869, when Père David, a French priest and scientist, came to China to collect samples of rare flowers and animals.

When he heard about the "white bear"—as the panda was called then—he ordered a native hunter to shoot one for him. Then the priest sent the skin and skeleton to the Paris Museum, along with a letter telling them everything he had learned about "the prettiest animal I know."

After museum workers studied the animal, they stuffed

A lifelike museum display

it to look like a live panda and displayed it. As the news
of this appealing new animal spread, museums in Europe
and America promptly sought pandas to add to their
collections.

To supply them, animal dealers and big game hunters rushed off to China. Once there, these strangers in a foreign land first had to learn where the pandas lived. When the men finally climbed the mountains into the misty bamboo forests, it was hard for them to find the animals. Still, a few Europeans found pandas, shot them, and sold the skins and skeletons to museums back home.

Two sons of President Theodore Roosevelt led the first American expedition to China to capture a panda. For weeks the group struggled through animal trails in the dense bamboo jungle. Even with the aid of several native hunters and dogs, all the men found were the animals' tracks.

Finally, after following new tracks for hours one day, they spied a panda slowly emerging from a hollow in a spruce tree. Both Roosevelts fired, as the animal ambled into the bamboo. They later gave its skin to the Field Museum in Chicago.

Soon zoos wanted live pandas. When young William Harkness decided to go to China, hoping to bring a panda back alive, it seemed as if he could succeed if

Red pandas

have huge teeth, eat bamboo, and have short intestines. But these two pandas not only look different, they also have very different habits.

Still other scientists now believe that the giant panda is neither a bear nor a raccoon, but that it belongs in a family of its own.

Chinese leopard

5

HOW THE GIANT PANDA LOOKS AND ACTS

A Chinese legend explains how the panda's fur became black and white. Long ago a girl grew up with several all-white pandas. One day when she was playing with them, a leopard attacked a baby panda. The brave girl tried to fight off the big cat, but she died of wounds the leopard inflicted.

Other pandas, hearing of her courage, came to the girl's home. To show their grief, they wore black on their arms, legs, and shoulders. When the pandas cried, whatever their tears touched became black, so adding black eyes, noses, and ears.

The panda's fur looks soft and fluffy to the eye, but

it feels stiff and coarse to the touch. This is bad news for people wanting its fur for coats, but good news for the panda. In fact, its fur doesn't even make a comfortable sleeping mat.

Its fur serves the animal well. The coarse outer hairs protect it against the cold, and a thick, oily undercoat acts to waterproof the panda in its wet jungle home.

Though pandas have massive heads and heavy bodies, they are remarkably flexible. They can turn and twist in many ways. They can scratch any part of their bodies whether they are sitting up or lying down.

While they can stand on their hind legs, they can't walk on them. Their two legs aren't strong enough to support their heavy bodies—even heavier than they seem because of the weight of their bones. They are twice as heavy as bones of most other animals of the same size.

Pandas walk in pigeon-toed fashion, with their front toes turned inward. They lumber along, swaying from

Yun-Yun, a female panda visiting the Los Angeles Zoo. The fur looks soft, but it is stiff and coarse.

side to side, with heads bent low. Because their rear legs are weaker than their front legs, pandas are likely to break into a trot only when chased. The hair-covered pads on their feet help them wander easily around icy slopes and over slippery rocks.

The animals have poor vision. But their excellent hearing and sense of smell are valuable aids to them in their forest home.

The Chinese call giant pandas "hermits of the forest" because they live alone most of their lives. Only during mating season or while mothers are with their cubs are pandas seen together.

They are usually gentle among themselves, but males may fight to win a female as a mate, In the wild pandas are also usually quiet, shy animals. To his surprise, George Schaller—an outstanding American scientist who was invited to China to study their pandas—found the young ones to be friendly and as easy to handle as pets.

Pandas walk in a pigeon-toed fashion.

6

THE PANDA'S FEEDING HABITS

In the wild pandas live almost entirely on bamboo. They may spend as many as sixteen hours a day eating it. They dine in long stretches, day and night, and rest in between.

A hungry panda sometimes sits down in the forest, grabs a stalk of bamboo close by and bends it. Then it brings the food to its mouth, much as people do. A "sixth claw" on each of the panda's forepaws acts as a thumb and enables the animal to grasp and hold the bamboo firmly.

Pandas prefer to munch on the more tender bamboo leaves and shoots, but they also tackle the tough stalks.

Hsing-Hsing, the National Zoological Park's male giant panda, chews bamboo with his mighty molars.

To break them up is a hard task even for a man with an ax. But pandas have no trouble crushing and chewing them. Their powerful jaw muscles and their huge teeth— about seven times the size of human teeth—make it easy.

However, pandas have trouble digesting bamboo, because they have short intestines. Much of the bamboo they consume doesn't have time to be digested. For sufficient nourishment, they must devour a huge amount of food. In one day a single panda may eat forty pounds of bamboo.

To add variety to their diets, pandas sometimes nibble on grass and wild flowers, and feast on mushrooms that pop up in the snow. In honey season they may wander down the slopes and raid a farmer's beehive.

Pandas are also carnivores, or flesh eaters. If they stumble on meat, they'll eat it, but they usually move too slowly to catch a mouse or any other small animal. Still, pandas can sometimes grab a fish from a mountain stream.

7

BIRTH AND GROWTH

A panda about to become a mother starts collecting nesting material in the forest and hunts for a snug, safe place for her baby. She usually chooses a tree hole, or another animal's deserted den or cave. Almost always she'll give birth to one or two cubs.

Quickly after her blind and helpless cub is born, the mother directs it to her nipples. When her little panda is hungry again, it signals its need with a cry much like a human baby's. At first the cub may cry for its mother's milk as often as twelve times a day.

Like bears, pandas are tiny at birth. They rarely weigh more than a four-ounce cube of butter, and are about

Giant panda den site in fir tree, Wolong Nature Reserve.

the size of a small kitten. With her huge paw the mother panda could cover her infant. She herself can weigh two hundred pounds—or eight hundred times the weight of her cub.

At first the cub looks like a little ball of white fur. Its black markings appear in one area at a time, and in one month the baby panda will have black ears, eye patches, legs, and shoulder band, just like its mother.

The panda is a caring mother. In these early days she rarely leaves her infant out of her arms. She hugs it against her warm body, licks it clean, and protects it from harm. When she leaves her hideaway, she carries her cub with her. If she has twins, she carries one in a paw, the other in her mouth.

In about two months a baby panda opens its eyes; another month and its first milk teeth begin to appear. As the little one gains strength, it climbs on its mother's back. She plays with it at times, tossing it from paw to paw, rolling it over and over, or wrestling with it. At seven months a panda may weigh twenty-five pounds, and it has begun to claw and climb trees.

Young pandas playing on the rocks.

Now the cub sometimes slips away from its mother and plays alone. One of its favorite games is tumbling a rock down a slope, then chasing after it. Catching up with the rock, the cub starts it rolling again.

In winter it may grab a frozen limb, break off an icicle from the limb, and keep batting the ice into the air until the ice melts. The cub also plays in the snow. It slides down a slope on its stomach, then it climbs back up the mountain and repeats the fun.

The cub still nurses, but now it also nibbles on the tender bamboo leaves. It doesn't sample the tough stalks until after its first birthday, when its strong permanent teeth begin to appear. Then it gives up drinking its mother's milk. When it starts on its bamboo diet, the cub weighs about sixty pounds.

More and more often it wanders away from its mother. The cub may try in vain to catch a mouse that skitters by. But even without any meat to eat the panda's weight may soar to a hundred pounds in the next six months. About this time the cub will slip away altogether from its mother to find a new home in the bamboo forest.

Thereafter, young female pandas usually feed and travel within a small area. Males select a much larger area—about two square miles—and sometimes their home overlaps those of several females.

Pandas can mate when they are six years old, sometimes earlier. To attract a female, the male climbs a tree in the spring and gives a loud, weird cry—the only time in the year he makes this sound. When a male and female find each other, and both are willing, they mate.

Afterward, the female drives off the male with a hard bite. Within four to six months she may give birth to a baby panda. Eighteen months later, when her cub leaves her, the mother returns to living alone.

As pandas grow older, they play less and sleep more. As they get heavier, they are unlikely to climb trees, except when chased by wild dogs. When it is necessary, they can wade across mountain streams.

When they reach their full growth, pandas are about five feet long. Females can weigh well over 200 pounds; males grow larger, and may weigh more than 250 pounds. Still, giant pandas are hardly "giants." It would take forty of them to weigh as much as one elephant.

8

LIFE IN THE ZOO

Some of the earliest pandas shipped overseas didn't survive the trip. Su-Lin, the first one that did, lived only fourteen months in the Brookfield Zoo. But as zoos learned more about taking care of pandas, the animals fared better. Chi-Chi, a London Zoo favorite, pleased the crowds there for fourteen years. And Li-Li has spent twenty-three years in the Peking Zoo.

Only about forty giant pandas have ever been seen outside China—all of them in zoos. Wherever they appeared, they've been extremely popular. Over 32 million people watched the antics of Lan-Lan in the Tokyo Zoo, and when he died, Japanese children prayed at the empty cage.

Ling-Ling climbing.

Some say that Emperor Hirohito of Japan, while visiting England, did not smile until he saw Chi-Chi, the first panda he had ever seen. As Dr. Reed of the National Zoo in Washington said, "Pandas can steal your heart away."

Each zoo panda has its own personality. From the

Hsing-Hsing reaches for an apple used for the snowman's eye.

beginning Ling-Ling ("cute little girl" in Chinese) was curious and playful, and liked crowds. Hsing-Hsing ("bright star" in Chinese) was shy, and slower to explore new surroundings. At times he disappeared into his den, hiding from onlookers.

Cubs are usually gentle and friendly, and they love to

The lazy way to eat bamboo.

have their keepers scratch their backs. But even young pandas can be dangerous. Ling-Ling in her first year here rushed at a keeper's legs. Luckily, his cowboy boots prevented the panda from sinking her teeth into his flesh. As zoo pandas grow older, they tend to become grumpy, and at times bad-tempered. One full-grown panda bit off the hand of its keeper.

In the zoo, as in the wild, bamboo is the panda's favorite food. But the animals have sampled and accepted many new items. While at the London Zoo, Chi-Chi especially liked roast chicken.

The two Washington pandas dine twice a day on a mixture of rice, cottage cheese, soy oil, and honey, enriched with vitamins and minerals. Every day they also eat twenty-five pounds of bamboo and snack between meals on carrots and apples. Once in a while they've gobbled up chocolate candy bars—a special treat to bribe the pandas to do something the keepers want them to do.

But at first zoos had to struggle to find enough nourishing foods that the pandas would eat. In time they did so well at the National Zoo that Ling-Ling and

Ying-Xin, a visiting panda, rolling in artificial snow in the San Francisco Zoo.

Hsing-Hsing became fat and flabby. When this happened, zoo keepers started feeding the pandas less food and watching their weight more carefully.

Very young and very old pandas sleep a great deal in zoos. They are not at all fussy about how they do it. They may sleep on their stomachs. They may sleep on their backs. Or they may doze off sitting against a fence, or even supported by a fork in a tree.

When they play they tumble, do headstands, somersaults, and climb around their log piles. Some spend hours rolling balls, hoops, and barrels.

Like children, zoo pandas sometimes destroy their toys. Ling-Ling and Hsing-Hsing quickly wrecked their first heavy rubber basketballs. When they were given other supposedly "panda-proof" basketballs, they wrecked them all, one by one. Now they are enjoying their new gym with tunnels, balance beams, and swings.

The two pandas have been housed next to each other in separate cages, but sometimes keepers allow them to play together. Zoo scientists worried that if the pair shared the same quarters all the time, they might fight. This did happen when two pandas were put into the same cage in a Japanese zoo.

9

ENDANGERED

Giant pandas are among the most endangered animals in the world. Some scientists think that there may be only one thousand in the wild. Others believe that only a few hundred now survive.

The Chinese consider their giant pandas a national treasure, partly because these appealing animals are so scarce. So it has been many years since they have allowed anyone to capture or buy a panda without permission.

Once, about a hundred years ago, in exchange for one giant panda, they asked an animal dealer to give them three giraffes, two zebras, two rhinoceros, and two hippopotamuses. More recently, they have parted with

Study area for giant panda research. Wolong Nature Reserve in Sichuan Province, China.

their pandas only as "gifts of friendship" to selected countries.

Pandas are so scarce that most farmers living in panda country have hardly ever seen one. And when George

Schaller began his study of pandas in China, two months slipped by before he saw a single panda.

To find the pandas, Schaller and the team of American and Chinese scientists he is working with set traps for them in open cages, using smoked meat as bait. When a panda reaches for it, the cage door slides down, catching it inside. Scientists then inject a harmless drug into the animal. When it is drowsy enough, they attach a radio collar around its neck.

Later, as the freed panda saunters around, its collar sends out signals for a year, giving the experts important information about what the panda is doing.

10

ENEMIES

Older pandas usually have little to fear from predators in the wild, but young pandas can be in danger. A leopard might seize a cub that had wandered away from its mother. Or a pack of wild dogs could capture a cub. Or if a mother left her tiny one in a tree, a hungry eagle might snatch it for its dinner.

For a time man hunted the pandas. Foreign explorers invaded their wilderness home searching for pandas until the Chinese outlawed hunting them.

But this did not end the panda's troubles. As the Chinese population exploded in this century, people kept overflowing into panda country. Farmers moving up into

49

Asiatic wild dog

their mountains cut down forests to provide land for their farms and lumber for their homes. As the bamboo disappeared, the panda's range kept shrinking.

The latest threat to the giant panda comes from a food shortage within the remaining bamboo forests. It began in 1975 when the life cycle of umbrella bamboo ended.

Each variety of bamboo lives only for a certain number of years. Then it flowers, withers, and dies everywhere, scattering seeds on the ground. As the seeds take root, the bamboo slowly grows again. But several years may go by before the pandas can depend on the growing bamboo for food.

In earlier times when bamboo forests rose all around them, pandas just traveled to other areas and ate other kinds of bamboo. As the forests shrunk, travel was no longer as easy. Even when the umbrella bamboo died, many of the pandas stayed where they were. Before long, almost 150 died of starvation. Now a recent die-off of arrow bamboo threatens the animals that survived.

Some of them have ambled down the slopes searching for food. They have eaten farmers' corn and wheat, raided their kitchens at night, and devoured peasants' lunches while they were working in the fields.

Yet the natives have not tried to harm the pandas. In times past when they raided beehives, the peasants wanted only to frighten them. So sometimes they merely waved blankets at the animals until they left. Now people

living near panda country are doing their best to provide food for their thin visitors.

Some farmers set out food each morning; others have killed goats for the pandas to eat; and young men have scaled mountain peaks to find bamboo for the starving animals. The Chinese government offers large rewards to anyone rescuing a panda.

Giant panda climbing a tree.

11

SAVING THE GIANT PANDA

Several countries are now spending millions of dollars in a joint effort to save the rare and endangered giant panda. Money is also coming from unusual sources. Chinese children have added their small coins. And when Nancy Reagan visited China recently, the first lady gave fourteen thousand pennies from American youngsters to the cause.

The Chinese government, of course, has led the movement to aid their suffering pandas, setting aside twelve areas as reserves for them. And the Chinese-American team of scientists has been studying the giant pandas in the wild since 1980 mostly to learn ways to help them survive.

Hsing-Hsing standing and Ling-Ling on the ground. Zoos have made great efforts to breed giant pandas in captivity.

Some of the pandas that George Schaller—the leader of the Americans—and his teammates capture are brought back to their research center. There in the Wolong Reserve their chief interest is to get the pandas to breed. When natural methods fail, as they often do, they try artificial means.

Schaller and the others on the Chinese-American team are also working on ways to solve the pandas' food crisis. They have left cooked pork chops on the slopes to lure pandas to move to other areas and try other kinds of bamboo. They have developed a new strain of bamboo. They are also testing various foods—such as winter wheat—that the panda may be able to eat instead of bamboo.

Zoos are also doing their part to save the giant pandas. They've been making great efforts to breed them, but as in the wild, there are problems. There are only a few days each spring when a female can mate and perhaps have cubs. It has not been easy for the experts to discover when these special days will occur.

Then, too, when males and females are brought

together, they often show no interest, and they may even snarl at each other. So it was when Chi-Chi, a female, was flown to Moscow to meet An-An, and again later when he visited Chi-Chi in the London Zoo.

It has been different with Ling-Ling and Hsing-Hsing. They get along well together, but seven years slipped by before Ling-Ling had a cub. Sadly, the tiny panda died within three hours of its birth. In 1984 a second cub was stillborn, disappointing the zoo again.

Pandas born in other zoos often haven't fared well either. When they give birth to twins, it isn't unusual for one to die soon afterward. And in Mexico City in 1980, Ying-Ying rolled over and crushed her tiny, week-old baby, the first panda to be born in captivity outside of the Orient.

Still, hard as it is, zoos haven't given up trying to breed pandas by natural methods. But like the Chinese-American team, zoos have also been experimenting with artificial ways. So far they have had only a little success.

Many problems need to be solved before the giant panda will be saved, but the Chinese intend to save it.

Hsing-Hsing following Ling-Ling.

Even with all the help from scientists in the wild and in zoos around the world, it won't be easy. As George Schaller says, "It will be a long-term effort. You can never let go." But no effort will be too great to assure that this wonderful animal will have a bright future.

INDEX